The Making of a Champion

An International Rugby Union Star

Heinemann
LIBRARY

Andrew Langley

H www.heinemann.co.uk/library

Visit our website to find out more information about **Heinemann Library** books.

To order:

☎ Phone 44 (0) 1865 888066

▤ Send a fax to 44 (0) 1865 314091

▭ Visit the Heinemann Bookshop at www.heinemann.co.uk/library to browse our catalogue and order online.

First published in Great Britain by Heinemann Library, Halley Court, Jordan Hill, Oxford OX2 8EJ, part of Harcourt Education. Heinemann is a registered trademark of Harcourt Education Ltd.

Editorial: Geoff Barker, Rebecca Hunter and Dan Nunn
Design: Ian Winton
Illustrations: Peter Bull and Stefan Chabluk
Picture Research: Rachel Tisdale
Consultant: Jim Foulerton
Production: Duncan Gilbert

Originated by Ambassador Litho Ltd
Printed in China by WKT Company Limited

ISBN 0 431 18939 0
08 07 06 05 04
10 9 8 7 6 5 4 3 2 1

British Library Cataloguing in Publication Data

Langley, Andrew

An international Rugby Union star – (The making of a champion)

1. Rugby Union football – Juvenile literature

2. Rugby football – Training – Juvenile literature

I. Title

796.3'33

A full catalogue record for this book is available from the British Library.

Acknowledgements

The publishers would like to thank the following for permission to reproduce photographs:

Empics pp. **7 top**, **13 top**, **13 bottom**, **19**, **20**, **21 top**, **21 bottom**, **23 top**, **27 bottom**, **32**, **36**, **37**, **38**, **41 top**; Getty Images pp. **4** (Mark Nolan), **5** (David Rogers), **8** (Martin Bureau), **9 top** (Nick Wilson), **9 bottom** (Craig Prentis), **10** (Alex Livesey), **11** (David Rogers), **12** (Alex Livesey), **14** (David Rogers), **15 top**, **15 bottom** (Shaun Botterill), **16** (Adam Pretty), **17** (Stuart Hannagan), **18** (David Rogers), **23 bottom** (David Rogers), **24** (Damien Meyer), **25 top** (William West), **25 bottom** & **26** (David Rogers), **27 top** & **28** (Adam Pretty), **29 top** (David Rogers), **29 bottom** (Touchline), **30** (Odd Andersen), **31 top** (Jamie McDonald), **31 bottom** (David Rogers), **33** (Nick Laham), **34** (Darren England), **35 top** (David Rogers), **35 bottom** (Nick Wilson), **39 top** (Matt Turner), **39 bottom** (Daniel Berehulak), **40** (Adam Pretty), **41 bottom** (David Rogers), **42** (Tony Ashby), **43 top** (Ross Kinnaird), **43 bottom** (Michael Cooper); The Mary Evans Picture Library pp. **6**, **7 bottom**.

Cover photograph reproduced with permission of Martin Bureau/AFP/Getty Images

Every effort has been made to contact copyright holders of any material reproduced in this book. Any omissions will be rectified in subsequent printings if notice is given to the publishers.

The paper used to print this book comes from sustainable resources.

Contents

Words printed in bold letters, **like these**, are explained in the Glossary.

This is rugby union

At its best, rugby union is one of the fastest and most thrilling games in the world. There are few more exciting sights in sport than a player crashing over the line to score a **try**, knocking over an opponent with a bone-shaking tackle, or sending a towering drop kick between the posts to snatch a victory in the final moments of a match. Still better is doing one of these things yourself!

A world sport

Thousands of people throughout the world play rugby union. Millions more watch the big matches live at the grounds or on television. It is a major sport in England, Wales, Scotland, Ireland, France and much of the rest of Europe, Australia, New Zealand, the Pacific islands and South Africa. It also has a big following in many other countries including Canada, Argentina, Japan and the USA. There are several international competitions in each region, the best-known being the Six Nations in Europe and the Super Sixes in the southern hemisphere. International teams play each other regularly, and the Rugby World Cup takes place every four years.

Joe Rokocoko of New Zealand hurtles towards the try line during the 2003 Rugby World Cup, while a French defender tries to stop him with a tackle.

A game for everyone

Anyone can enjoy rugby, because there is a place for people of all shapes and sizes. People with a short or slight build can play as one of the **backs**, because speed and cunning are more important here than sheer bulk. France's former scrum half Fabien Galthie is a fine example of this. The **forwards** are usually bigger – the tallest play in the second row, the fastest in the back row, and the shortest in the **front row**.

Rugby includes a huge variety of activities. You can catch, throw, kick and run with the ball. If your opponent has the ball, you can tackle, push, pull or try to wrestle it from him. Additional skills are needed for **set-piece** play.

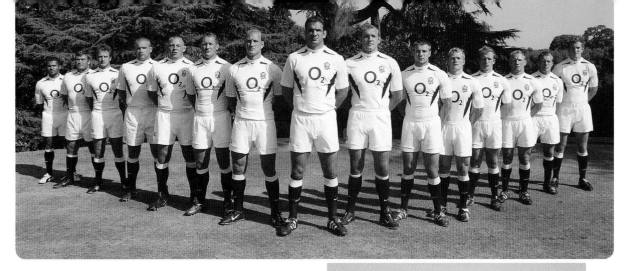

Brawn and brains

Rugby is a game of physical contact. This is often hard and painful, and always challenging, especially in tackling and playing in the **scrum**. But rugby players need to be intelligent as well as tough. There are always plenty of options for the next move to make on the field – to run, to kick, to pass, to support – and the best players are those who consistently choose the right ones.

Champions of the rugby world! The England team lines up for the photographer before flying out to compete in the 2003 World Cup in Australia – which they won!

Rugby union is also one of the great team sports, in which everybody contributes to a victory. Players cannot win a game on their own, no matter how brilliant they are. They depend on the work and support of the 14 other team members.

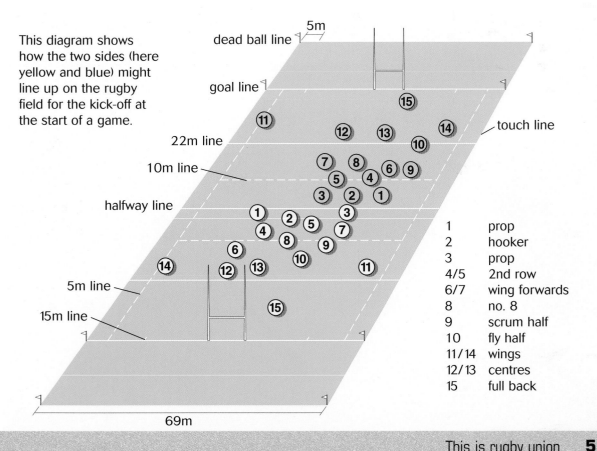

This diagram shows how the two sides (here yellow and blue) might line up on the rugby field for the kick-off at the start of a game.

dead ball line
5m
goal line
touch line
22m line
10m line
halfway line
5m line
15m line
69m

1	prop
2	hooker
3	prop
4/5	2nd row
6/7	wing forwards
8	no. 8
9	scrum half
10	fly half
11/14	wings
12/13	centres
15	full back

The running game

According to legend, the game of rugby was invented by someone breaking the rules. He was a schoolboy named William Webb Ellis, and one day in 1823 he was playing a game of football at Rugby School in Warwickshire, England. To the outrage of the referee (and the other players) he picked the ball up and ran with it. A new type of ball game had been born, and it has been known as 'rugby' football ever since.

Making the rules

In fact, rugby also developed from the free-for-all form of football which had been played in Europe since the Middle Ages. Whole villages would compete against each other using a blown-up pig's bladder as a ball. The heaving mass of rival villagers would kick and run and wrestle and punch as they tried to get the ball into their opponents' stronghold. From this, both rugby and ordinary football emerged.

By the middle of the 19th century, rugby had become very popular in Britain. But it was still a violent and chaotic game, with no proper rules or organization. In 1871 a number of English clubs got together to form the first rugby union, playing under a uniform set of rules. Unions were set up in Scotland, Ireland and Wales soon afterwards.

Boys at Rugby School scramble after the ball (and scare the spectators) in this print from 1870.

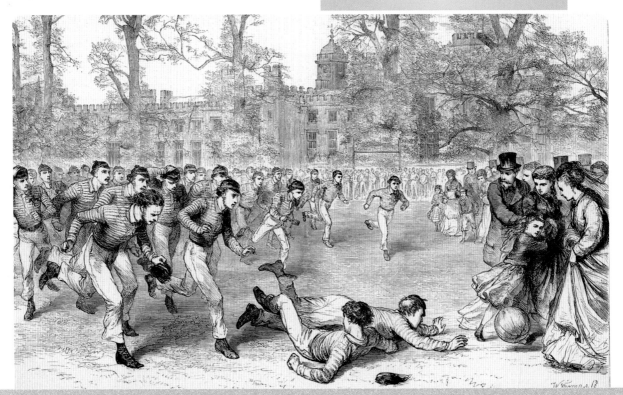

Internationals and professionals

The game under rugby union rules spread rapidly. The very first international match also took place in 1871, between Scotland and England in Edinburgh (the Scots won). Ireland and Wales joined the competition, and in 1891 a combined British and Irish side (later known as the 'British Lions') made a tour of South Africa. Over the next two decades, teams from France, New Zealand, South Africa and Australia visited the UK.

Rugby union football grew into a major world sport very slowly. It was a game played entirely by amateurs, who were not allowed to accept any kind of payment. They worked in full-time jobs during the rest of the week. By the 1980s, however, many new nations were joining the international circuit. These included Argentina, Romania, Japan and the Pacific teams of Tonga, Fiji and Samoa. Then, in 1995, came the biggest change of all when rugby union went professional. Now players could be paid salaries, and devote themselves entirely to the sport.

This illustration shows a Victorian rugby player in the late 19th century.

Rugby has now spread to all parts of the world. This action is from a match between Wales and Japan in 2001.

Rugby League fact

Rugby soon split into two main types or 'codes'. Payment of players had always been banned, but in 1893 several clubs in northern England broke away from the English Rugby Union so that they could go professional. They formed the Rugby League, and developed different rules (for instance, having 13 instead of 15 players in a team). Rugby League has since flourished in many parts of the world – especially where the Union game is also played. Over the years, many union players joined the league so that they could earn a living from it. But since the professional era began in 1995 the flow has been reversed, with league stars such as Australian Mat Rogers signing for union teams.

Rugby around the world

Like cricket, rugby union was first established in the UK and many of the countries of what was then the British Empire. Rugby union was especially popular in Australasia, South Africa and the Pacific, but (unlike cricket) never caught on in the Indian sub-continent or the Caribbean. Today it is a truly worldwide sport, with its own World Cup. This was first held in 1987, and has taken place every four years since then. The International Rugby Board now has over 90 member countries.

Europe

The major competition in Europe is the Six Nations Championship, contested each year between England, Ireland, Scotland, Wales, France and newcomers Italy. Several other European countries are bidding to join this elite group, notably Romania, Georgia and Russia. These and many other sides also take part in the European Nations Tournament.

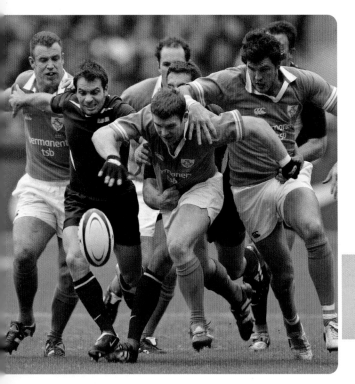

Oceania

New Zealand and Australia have traditionally been by far the strongest rugby nations in the world (though in recent years they have been challenged by South Africa, France and England). New Zealand, Australia and South Africa compete with each other in the annual Tri-Nations tournament. Rugby is also very strong in some Pacific islands, which play regular **Test** matches against major sides. Tonga and Fiji have recorded wins over Australia.

Asia

Rugby in Asia is confined mostly to the Far East, where Japan is the leading side. Japan qualified for the second stage of the 2003 World Cup, easily defeating South Korea and Taiwan in the process.

Irish player Gordon d'Arcy (centre) kicks the ball forward during a Six Nations match between Ireland and France in 2004.

Africa

South Africa has been a major rugby nation for over 100 years. The side was excluded from the international scene during the 1970s and 1980s because of the nation's **apartheid** policy. But since then major efforts have been made to create a fair and integrated team. South Africa won the World Cup in 1995. Rugby union is now also gaining ground in Zimbabwe, Kenya and other African countries.

Americas

In recent years the popularity of rugby has soared in Canada, though many leading players go overseas to earn a living. Continued success in the 2003 World Cup has made the game stronger in North America (the USA also appeared in the latter stages of the 1999 competition). Argentina and Uruguay are the leading rugby union sides in South America.

'Sevens' (matches played with only seven players on each side) are very popular throughout the world. Here Usaia Mataki of Fiji carries the ball during a game against New Zealand in the Hong Kong Sevens tournament of 2002.

Women's world champions

The New Zealand women's rugby team is even more successful than the men's. The 'Black Ferns' won the 2002 World Cup in Spain, beginning with a 117-0 victory over Germany and ending by beating England 19-9 in the final. Their outstanding player in the final was **scrum** half Monique Hirovanaa, who ran half the length of the pitch to score her decisive **try**. The chairman of the International Rugby Board said afterwards that women's rugby was 'one of the world's fastest-growing sports'. The women's game is certainly flourishing in the major rugby nations of the world, whilst many new nations are also emerging, including Trinidad and Sweden.

Starting young

It is vital to learn the basic skills of rugby union properly from the beginning. Once players know the correct techniques of passing, handling and kicking an oval ball, they have the ideal foundation for playing the game well. This will depend largely on the coaching they get from an early age. One reason for rugby's growing popularity throughout the world is that there are plenty of adults (paid and unpaid) who give their time to training the youngest generations of players.

Rugby in and out of school

Children usually begin playing the game at the age of six or seven. If their school does not have an under-7s team, then there will probably be one at a junior club nearby. At this early stage, players take part in Mini Rugby. This is the simplest form of the game, taking place on a small section of a full-sized pitch. There are seven players per side, and no physical contact or kicking is allowed, so that there is no danger of injury at such an early stage.

Young players take part in a Mini Rugby Festival in London.

Joe van Niekerk

The South African back row star Joe van Niekerk is a perfect example of schools coaching at its best. Born in Port Elizabeth in 1980, van Niekerk was an outstanding schoolboy player and by the age of 17 was captain of the South Africa Schools team. A year later he was picked for the national Under-19 side, and went on to captain the South Africa Under-21s. By early 2002 he was a regular member of the full Springbok (South African) team, and scored an amazing **try** against Samoa. Soon afterwards he was chosen as one of the five International Rugby Board (IRB) Players of the Year.

Learning the basics

Great care should be taken to introduce the more physically demanding parts of the game slowly and safely. By the age of eight, players are learning to tackle properly, but there are still no full **scrums** or **lineouts**. At eleven, they are given their first taste of scrummaging (**binding** and packing down against their opponent's scrums at a **set-piece**), with a team made up of five forwards and seven backs. At thirteen they progress to Junior Rugby with full 15-player teams. Even at this stage, lineouts (receiving a throw-in from the touchline) should be restricted to two players, with a ban on the lifting of the player jumping by other players.

Junior club teams

At the age of about eighteen, full-on rugby begins. The best players are picked for their age-group teams as they grow up, from under-14s to under-19s. Many schools have a strong and well-organized rugby programme involving matches against neighbouring teams. Otherwise, young people can find out about local clubs with junior teams. Young players should choose those clubs which have regular coaching sessions for younger sides, and a carefully planned process for promoting players as they get older.

Equipment and clothing

A team's colours mean a lot. Think of the all-black kit of New Zealand, the gold of Australia, the green of Ireland and the white of England. But rugby clothing and equipment have a bigger role to play than just increasing team spirit. They can make a big difference to a player's performance on the field and in training, and (even more importantly) protect against serious injuries and strains.

Team strip and boots

Most teams wear shirts and shorts made of cotton or polyester. Some players like to have short sleeves and some – mainly in the Pacific – have no sleeves at all. Shorts should have both an elasticized waist and a tie cord so that they can be adjusted to the correct tightness. In cold or wet weather, some players also wear special heat-retaining undershorts which keep the leg muscles supple.

A good-fitting and high quality pair of boots is vital. Modern lightweight boots are made of a combination of leather and plastic, and have inner soles which give stiffness to the middle of the foot, and more softness at the front so that the toes can stay flexible. Most boots have eight studs, which must not be longer than 18 millimetres.

Protecting the body

From a young age, rugby players are advised to wear protective clothing underneath their shirts. Vest tops, with light foam shoulder pads, are contoured to fit the body and guard areas most likely to be injured. Women players should wear protector bras or combined shoulder and breast protection.

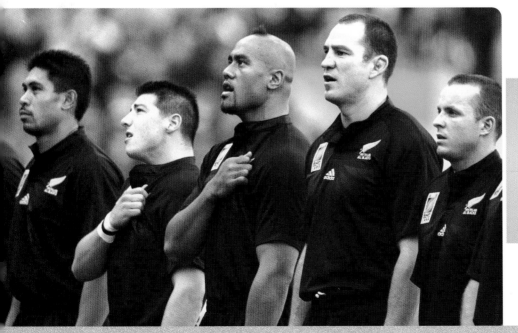

New Zealand players line up to sing their national anthem before a match in 1999. They are wearing their famous 'All Black' shirts and shorts.

The head is the most vulnerable part of the body, especially in a high-impact sport like rugby. Some **forwards** (especially in the front and second rows of the **scrum**) protect their ears with layers of tape. Many more use headguards which are moulded to cover the tops of their heads as well as the ears. A few **backs**, such as the Irishman David Humphreys, also wear headguards.

Early rugby balls

The first rugby ball was a pig's bladder, as we have already seen. But the first kind of ball made especially for the game was leather, with a rubber bladder inside to hold the air. Laces in the leather tightened up the slit where the air valve was. Leather balls could be heavy and slippery – even more so when they were sodden with water and mud!

A modern rugby union ball is very different. It has a polyester skin covered with cotton, and a synthetic rubber coating on top which makes it easy to grip.

The ball fact

The ball should weigh between 400 and 440 grams, and the length between the pointed ends should be 280 to 300 millimetres. Smaller sizes are used for Mini Rugby and Junior Rugby.

England's Danny Grewcock is a second-row forward and wears a scrumcap to protect his head.

Running and passing

Running and handling the ball are the two most basic skills of a rugby player. After all, the main object of a game is to score **tries** by grounding the ball over the opponents' try line. Running sounds simple, but includes a huge variety of possibilities (such as running to support teammates). Handling, too, involves many different actions, from catching and passing to picking the ball up from the ground and releasing it when tackled.

Straight or crooked?

The player with the ball should always aim to run straight, unless he or she needs to avoid a tackler ahead. After all, this is the shortest way to the opposing try line. It also gives colleagues the simplest choices in running to give support. The ball can be carried in one or both hands. With both hands, it is easier to pass to a teammate. But players can run faster with the ball in one hand, and have the other free to **hand off** (push away) opponents.

The aim of the runner is to get past opposing players. This can be done in several ways. To start with, the runner can aim to receive his pass when running at an angle which catches the opposition by surprise. Then there are the classic techniques for deceiving single tacklers. The runner can swerve away at the last moment, or 'side-step' by slowing down and then pushing his body sideways with a thrust of the opposite leg. The biggest trick of all is the dummy pass, when the runner pretends to pass to a teammate, but keeps hold of the ball while the tackler hesitates.

Georgia Stevens of England (with the ball) gives a perfect example of a 'hand off' to an opponent during a women's match against Spain in 2003.

Moving the ball

Rugby is above all a team game, and passing the ball among team members is the main way of keeping the action moving. The runner aims to pass the ball to someone who is in a better position. The whole body should be used in the action of passing, to give the ball more force and distance, and the pass should be timed to reach the receiver at speed somewhere between chest and waist.

There are many other types of pass for different situations. A scrum half may 'dive pass' from a scrum or **lineout**, to make the ball travel further and faster. A runner who is tackled may pass the ball with one hand even as he is falling. Or he can lob the ball high over the heads of opponents to reach a teammate.

Jason Robinson

Jason Robinson of England is one of the most exciting runners the game has ever seen. He is not only very fast, with explosive acceleration, but also a brilliant side-stepper and swerver. This is because he has a low centre of gravity and extraordinary strength and agility in his legs. These assets allow him to stay balanced on his feet and change from moving forward to moving sideways in a split second.

Tackling and broken play

Rugby union can be a messy game. Each side wants possession of the ball, and so aims to disrupt their opponents' moves. Tackles, interceptions, mauls (wrestling for the ball) and rucks (trying to push the other side off a grounded ball) can force people to make mistakes. The ball gets dropped, or knocked forward (which is against the rules), or carelessly given to the other team. The best players, such as New Zealander Richie McCaw, are those who can deal with broken and untidy play like this, and use it to their advantage.

Australia's Matt Burke has the ball but he is tackled by an Argentinian forward who has grabbed him from behind.

Making the hits

Tackling is central to a team's defensive strategy. Every player must have the skill, courage and confidence to be able to tackle effectively – and often. In senior matches, coaches often count the number of 'hits' made by each player on the opposition. These do not have to be massive 'crash' tackles. A well-timed and effective tackle is usually the safest.

Players should aim to tackle an opponent as soon as he or she receives the ball. This makes it more difficult for them to pass the ball on. Tackles are made from the front, side-on or from behind. Tacklers should always try to hit the ball carrier with their shoulders at a point which can bend or give – just above the knees, or in the stomach. In either case, the tackler's arms should be wrapped round the opponent's body, stopping him from moving or preventing him from passing the ball.

Recycling the ball

When players are tackled, it is important that they keep the ball in their team's possession. This means that they must pass it, allow a teammate to take it or take the ball to the ground (in this case it must be

The gain line fact

Everyone knows that there are white lines marked on a rugby field. But there are also lines which are not marked. One of the most important is the gain line. This is an imaginary line going across the pitch and through the centre of the point where play has stopped because of a scrum, maul, ruck or lineout. Each side wants to get across the gain line with the ball in their hands. Only by doing this will they have 'gained' ground and gone forward.

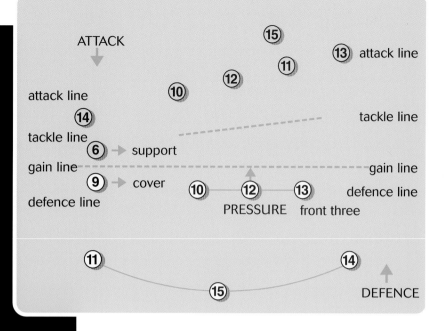

One England player holds the ball (centre) as the other forwards bind onto him and move forward against their French opponents. The ball carrier is still on his feet, so this is a 'maul'.

released immediately). But this will only work properly if other team members give support to the ball carrier. Everyone must know exactly what is expected of them.

At this point, open play has broken down, and what is called the 'second phase' begins. Possession of the ball can be won or lost here. If the ball carrier is on his feet, teammates form a 'maul' by **binding** round him, supporting him on each side. The opposition will try to rob him of the ball. If the ball carrier is on the ground, the ball is released and the players bind together to form a loose **scrum** called a 'ruck' and try to hook it back to the scrum half who can pass it to the backs.

Forward play

A strong team must have a strong set of **forwards**. These are the eight players at the front, whose job is to get possession of the ball at **set-pieces** (the **scrum** and the **lineout**, for example) and in broken play (usually rucks and mauls). If one set of forwards is consistently winning the set scrums and lineouts, their team will probably win the game. Their success will give their **backs** what is called 'good ball' – passing the ball to them and allowing lots of time and space to attack. This will put pressure on the opponents, who are likely to lose confidence and make mistakes.

The scrum

A set-piece scrum takes place after an infringement of the rules. Each set of forwards **binds** together in a well-organized formation. Then the two sides push against each other, while the scrum half (on the non-infringing team) places the ball in the centre of the scrum. In a good scrum, all eight forwards work as a unit, but each has a special job to do. In the **front row**, the **hooker** guides the ball back with his foot. He is supported by the two **props**, and together they take the impact of the opposing scrum. They also have to transfer the force of the two second row players who are

Jason Leonard

The **front row** is probably the toughest place to play in rugby. So former England prop Jason Leonard's achievement of winning a world-record 114 international caps, before announcing his retirement during the 2004 Six Nations, is an astonishing one. His first **Test** was in 1990 against Argentina, and since then he has battled it out with the greatest props in the game and come out on top. Leonard, seen here in the centre with the ball, has also overcome serious injuries. In 1992 he had to have a bone-graft to repair a disc in his neck. One of Leonard's greatest moments came in a Lions' match in New Zealand, when he and the pack pushed the rampaging All Blacks off their line at a set scrum.

pushing behind them. The job of the second row is to shove the whole scrum forwards and the opponents back.

The three back row players also push in the scrum. They help to bind (hold) together the two locks (second row forwards) in front, and to channel the ball back to the waiting scrum half. But they have other jobs. The no.8 (who binds in the middle) may pick up the ball from the back of the scrum and link with the backs. The two flankers (who bind on either side of the no.8) break early from the scrum to support their backs, or tackle the opposition backs as swiftly as possible. They should be first to the ball when play breaks down.

South Africa's Bakkies Botha is helped into the air by two team-mates as he catches the ball at a lineout against England in the 2003 World Cup.

The lineout

When one team puts the ball into **touch**, the other team puts it back into play at a lineout (see diagram on left). The two sets of forwards line up a metre apart and the thrower (usually the hooker) stands on the touch line exactly where the ball went out. He throws the ball in the air down the gap between the forwards, trying to make sure that it reaches the catcher on his own team. The catcher jumps to catch the ball, usually held up by supporting players so that he can get as high as possible. His opponents also try to catch the ball. Once it is caught, the ball can be thrown straight back to the scrum half, or held by the forwards until the scrum half calls for it.

A typical lineout

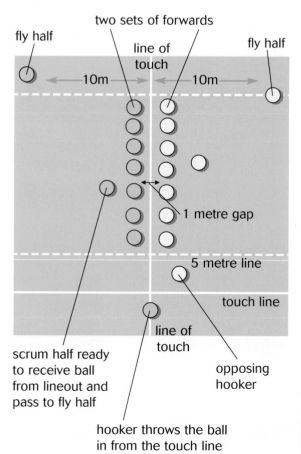

fly half

two sets of forwards

line of touch

fly half

10m

10m

1 metre gap

5 metre line

touch line

line of touch

scrum half ready to receive ball from lineout and pass to fly half

opposing hooker

hooker throws the ball in from the touch line

Back play

Broadly speaking, the **forwards** are the ball-getters and the **backs** are the ball-users. The main job of the seven backs is to receive the ball from the **scrums** and other set pieces and create opportunities for scoring. The backs are usually the fastest and most elusive runners, though they also have a vital defensive role in coping with attacks from the opposing back line.

South Africa's Joost van der Westhuizen has taken the ball from his forwards and dived to pass it out to the backs.

Meet the backs

The half backs (scrum half and fly half) are the links between backs and forwards. The scrum half (who is often the smallest player in the team) must have a long and accurate pass, to send the ball quickly to the backs. But he or she must also be able to make quick decisions about whether to pass, run with the ball or leave it with the forwards.

The fly half needs to be just as good at making tactical decisions, swiftly deciding whether to pass the ball on, or to kick it up the field, or to kick it into **touch**. He or she is the best kicker in the team, and usually takes the **set-piece** place-kicks.

The two centres must be fast movers and expert passers of the ball. They operate in the middle of the field – probably the best place to start an attack which will break through the opponent's defence. Outside them, on each side of the field, are the two wings, who should be the fastest and most deceptive runners. Wings usually score more tries than any other player.

A full back needs to be brave. Here Australia's Matt Burke leaps to catch a high ball even though he is surrounded by Irish forwards.

Last of all comes the full back. This position demands a rich combination of skills – at covering and tackling as the last line of defence, at catching high balls safely as opposing players thunder towards them, at kicking for touch, and at joining the back line to create an extra pair of hands at unexpected moments.

Moving the ball

A ball can always move faster than a player, so the speed and timing of passing along a line of backs can do much to create an attacking opportunity. But backs have many other passing tricks to try and deceive the opposition. They can use the 'miss-move', a very long pass which misses out one of the line, so getting the ball out more quickly. Or they can use the **scissors**, when the ball carrier twists to give the ball to another player running at a different angle.

Jonah Lomu

One of the greatest wings in rugby history, Lomu was also one of the biggest. Weighing 118 kg, and 1.96m in height, he also possessed lightning speed and enormous strength. This allowed him to smash through the opposition in a way that few other players have ever done. Lomu became the youngest ever All Black when he made his New Zealand debut in 1994 aged eighteen, and went on to score 35 tries in 60 internationals, including four in one game against England in the 1995 World Cup semi-final.

Kicking

It is against the rules to throw the ball forward, but you can kick it forward (or sideways or backwards). Kicking is one of the most important of rugby's basic skills. It is vital not only for scoring points (from drop kicks on the **half-volley**, and place kicks from still positions), but also in defence and attack (from **punt** kicks in which the player drops the ball from the hand and kicks it before it hits the ground).

Kicking for points

The place kick (see below) is used to start or re-start a game, or to score goals. The player places the ball upright or slightly tilted on the ground (in the old days, kickers made a small hole in the turf to hold the ball, but today they usually use a plastic support called a tee). Then he or she steps back a few paces, runs up and kicks. Place kickers are crucial members of a team, and generally score the most points, with penalty goals worth 3 points and the conversions of tries worth an 2 extra points.

Balance and concentration are vital for a successful drop kick.

For a drop kick (see above), the player drops the ball point downwards and kicks it as it touches the ground. The drop kick can be used to score a drop goal (3 points) in open play, or to re-start a game from the centre or the 22-metre line.

From a place kick or goal kick, the ball has to go between the posts and over the cross bar to score points.

Jonny Wilkinson

At the age of eleven, Jonny Wilkinson decided his ambition was to win a grand slam (every game in a Six Nations tournament) with the England rugby team. Ten years later, he had become England's highest-ever points scorer (passing the 400 mark), and one of the most consistent kickers ever seen. By September 2003 he had taken that total to 704 points in only 46 international games, with about 90 percent of his kicks being successful. The crowning moment of his career came when he played a central part in England's victory in the 2003 World Cup Final with a last-minute drop goal.

Kicking for position

The punt kick can be used for anything except scoring or starting a game. It is most commonly a defensive weapon. A player can take play quickly away from the danger area near his **try**-line by kicking the ball into **touch** as far as possible up the field. Or he can put pressure back on the other team by kicking over their heads into empty space behind.

A punt can also be used in this way to launch an attack, forcing opponents to turn and chase back towards their own line. A clever kick across the field can change the angle of the attack and catch opponents off-guard. An **up-and-under** is kicked very high into the air – this makes it more difficult for the opposition to catch, and also gives attacking players more time to reach the place where it lands. In a similar way, the chip kick is a short punt which goes over the heads of the approaching tacklers, and can then be gathered by the attackers.

Drop goals can win matches. Jannie De Beer kicks one of the five he scored for South Africa in their victory over England in the 1999 World Cup quarter-final.

Coaching

Rugby, like all sports, is developing and changing all the time. Since rugby union went professional in 1995 this process has got even faster. Teams are generally fitter and stronger than ever before, and **tactics** and training are more complex. On top of all this is the enormous increase in the number of matches top players are expected to take part in. High-quality coaching is needed to set and keep up these standards in skill, fitness and attitude.

Techniques and tactics

One of the basic jobs of a coach is to improve his players' skills and performance on the field. Big clubs usually have a coaching team, led by the chief coach but including specialists who teach kicking, scrummaging, back play and other individual **techniques**.

It is up to the coach to set targets for the players to achieve, and to correct any problems. First of all, of course, the problems have to be identified. This can be done both by close observation of the team during a game, and by studying video recordings of players in action afterwards. Some coaches even compile special videos for each player, showing their best and worst moments. Computer analysis can be used in a similar way, to build models of tactical plans, and to process statistics about activities such as tackle counts and passes. Coaches also use this technology to pinpoint the strengths and weaknesses of the opposite team.

Creating a team

Improving team spirit can do a lot to improve performance. A good coach will concentrate on making his players feel better about themselves, and listen to their personal concerns.

France's head coach Bernard Laporte (on the right) leads a training session with his team in 2003.

New Zealand coach John Mitchell (left) answers a question from a journalist at a press conference in Melbourne during the 2003 World Cup competition.

Every team member should know exactly what their role is, and should be encouraged to discover their own solutions to problems. Above all, rugby players should enjoy the game.

Most teams have a weekly discussion at which they talk about the previous weekend's match. The coach should encourage every player to say something, and should ask them what they have learned, and what area of their skills they need to work on. This makes everyone feel a valued member of the team.

Clive Woodward

Clive Woodward was an exceptional player, winning 21 caps at centre for England as well as representing the British Lions. After retirement from the game he became a successful businessman before turning to rugby coaching. He worked his way up the ladder, from local team Henley Rugby Club to national league clubs London Irish and Bath until in 1997 he was appointed as the first ever National England Rugby Union Coach. Since then the England team has been sensationally successful, achieving the highest reward of winning the World Cup in 2003. Woodward's techniques have been painstaking and refreshing – especially his policy of encouraging players to be flexible and try out new positions on the field. He is an outstanding motivator with a simple attitude to rugby union: 'It's got to be fun. People have got to enjoy the job.'

Practice

All world-class players have to practise hard and regularly. Coaches plan all practice sessions carefully, with specific tasks set out beforehand. The coach brings the players together and tells them exactly what they must aim to achieve during the session. The whole of the squad should be included in this programme, and everyone should be urged to make constructive comments. After a discussion, the players warm up and exercise, and then concentrate on sharpening their individual and group skills.

Handling drills

All players have to handle the ball. So, no matter which position they play in, all players should try to improve their handling skills – the **prop** in passing the ball like a centre, the centre in being able to rip the ball from an opponent like a prop, and so on. Drills for improving handling are usually done unopposed (without any opposition), or in small groups, and end with a short game of touch (no-tackling) rugby.

Obviously, the **backs** will practise passing the ball down the line, aiming to improve rhythm, speed and accuracy. They will also practise special moves, such as switching direction or 'looping' the ball. The **forwards** have their own handling skills to practise, including 'bunch' passing (close passing of the ball in a group, while moving up the field). Players should learn to give support all the time, and put themselves into good positions to receive a pass.

Tackle bags fact

Tackling is one of the most important areas of practice. But it is also the one most likely to cause bruising and other injuries – especially when routines are repeated many times. To lessen the risk, teams use special protective equipment such as the tackle bag, a large plastic sack filled with material which absorbs the shock of impact. One player holds this up while another tackles it. As an alternative, players can wear padded suits called 'body armour' for tackling practice.

Tackling practice. Jason Robinson (left) crashes into a tackle bag as he trains with the England squad in 2003.

During a practice session in 2003, Australian captain George Gregan (centre) passes the ball to a teammate.

Drills for set pieces

There are several **set-piece** moments in a rugby match. These include the kick-off, re-starts (from the centre, after a score, or from the 22-metre line), penalty kicks at goal, **scrums** and **lineouts**. Each one is an opportunity to take the advantage and gain ground, and has to be carefully prepared for.

Forwards usually practise the **binding** and pushing for the set scrum against a scrummage machine. This is a padded barrier on a spring which can be set to resist different levels of shoving. The machine is the best place to sort out matters of **technique**, and to help the scrum to act as a single unit. The lineout needs intensive coaching for individuals such as the jumpers. More complicated moves, such as shortening the line (taking players out) or **peeling**, need frequent practice.

The Fiji forwards push against a scrummage machine – watched by the backs.

Fitness

Many years ago, players in the Ireland team used to joke that they got fit by going for a run round the fly half (a large fellow called Barry McGann). The attitude to fitness and health, even among many internationals, was very relaxed. Today, this aspect has changed completely, and fitness training takes up a big part of a player's life. Most senior teams spend at least seven weeks before the start of the season improving fitness as well as practising their skills.

The training programme

A fit team can win matches by keeping up its work rate and producing spells of exceptional energy – especially at the beginning and end of each half. The aim of a fitness programme is to improve the players' strength, stamina and speed. Modern technology allows coaches to keep a close watch on their players' health (by monitoring heart rate, lung capacity and muscle mass for example). Each player can then be given an exercise regime to suit their individual fitness needs.

The basic programme includes distance running to build up stamina (endurance). All Black **forward** Graham Mourie used to run over 100 kilometres every week in the early part of the season. Other running exercises are aimed at improving acceleration, from a standing start or a jog to an explosive sprint. This practice at sudden changes of pace is an ideal preparation for the variations that happen in a real game.

Players must do regular exercises to increase their strength – whatever position they play in. 'Circuits' or sets of exercises focus on different muscle areas, such as the stomach, the calves, the thighs and the pectorals (chest muscles). Training with weights is also vital, but should only be done under the guidance of a specialist coach.

Stephen Larkham of Australia works out in the gym as he aims for peak fitness during the 2003 World Cup.

The England squad takes part in warm-up exercises before a full training session.

Illegal drugs fact

Drugs that artificially improve a player's performance, or increase muscle mass, are banned by rugby union authorities. During the 2003 World Cup, for example, regular checks were made to make sure they were not being used. After every game, two players from each side were asked to provide urine samples for testing. This programme continued throughout the year, so that over 500 players were tested. In future, the testing will also be extended to Under-21 and Under-19 sides.

Maintaining fitness

As well as keeping to a strict exercise programme, players must look after their bodies. They should spend at least thirty minutes warming up before a game, stretching and warming each set of muscles in turn.

They should eat a carefully designed, healthy diet, which contains regular portions of fresh vegetables and fruit, and avoids fatty 'fast' foods. Most coaches make sure their players eat plenty of carbohydrates (found in pasta, bread and potatoes) to give them energy before a match.

Upper body strength is vital for a rugby forward. Here Corne Krige and John Smit of South Africa train with weights in the gym to develop their muscles.

Injuries

Rugby is a high-impact sport. Bodies crash into each other, muscles are strained to the limit, and limbs can get into strange and dangerous positions. The pressures inside a set **scrum**, for instance, can be enormous, with as much as 1800 kilograms of body weight in motion. The wear and tear on top players has increased hugely in recent years, with stronger and heavier players and an almost non-stop programme of matches around the world.

First aid

Head injuries are usually the most serious. After a bad blow to the head, a player should always be taken off and checked for signs of concussion (dizziness or the possibility of becoming unconscious). Bleeding cuts to the head (or any other part of the body) should also be treated immediately off the field to prevent infection. Substitute players (called 'blood substitutes') are allowed to take the injured player's place until they are ready to resume.

Strained muscles and ligaments, and heavy bruising, are usually treated with ice packs straight after the game, in order to bring down the swelling. Players – even those with minor bumps and bruises – often soak in cold tubs when they come off the field for the same reason. Fractured or broken limbs, of course, need treatment in the accident and emergency ward of the local hospital.

Long-term treatment

Every team has a physiotherapist, who treats injuries both during the game on the field and during the week. The 'physio' starts by examining the injury, and then deciding the best way of speeding up the body's natural healing process.

Namibian player Ronaldo Pedro is carried off strapped onto a stretcher after being injured during a World Cup match against Australia in 2003.

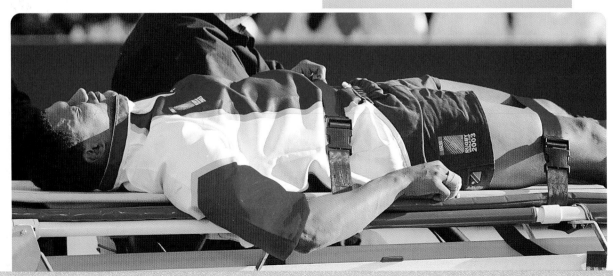

A physiotherapist treats an injury to the arm of Scotland's captain Bryan Redpath.

This can be helped by a variety of therapies, from massage with the hands to ultrasound treatment (using very high sound frequencies). The physio must also assess how long each injury will take to recover.

Preventing injury is just as important as curing it. A great deal of research has been done into injury prevention, and the results have been put into the fitness programmes of many teams. For instance, it was found that players with greater leg strength were less likely to suffer strains and pulled muscles, so special leg strengthening exercises were developed.

England's Lawrence Dallaglio enjoys a cold tub as part of a 'hot and cold' treatment after a game against New Zealand in 2003.

Injuries fact

A medical team kept a record of all Australian international matches between 1994 and 2000 and noted the number and types of injuries. In the 91 Tests during that period there were 143 injuries — about 1.5 per game. The majority of these were to the head (cuts and concussion) or to the knees and legs. The team also recorded the times of these injuries. They found that most occurred during the 20 minute period after half-time, when players were beginning to get tired.

Compete!

Rugby union is a game to be enjoyed. The best way to enjoy it is to play to the best of one's ability. This means having the correct attitude. A player must put in as much effort as possible, not only on the pitch but also during training and whenever he or she is representing a club or a nation. Of course, there is no point in playing if the team is not aiming to win – but it must compete fairly and sportingly.

A team game

A match cannot be won by one player on their own. A victory is a victory for the whole team, operating together. So players must all have confidence in themselves and in their teammates. If things go wrong, they should not make excuses or blame other people. By remaining positive in their attitude, they will find it easier to withstand pressure on and off the field.

The confidence and positive attitude should be reflected in a team's approach to a game. A former England coach, Jim Greenwood, put this approach simply into three vital points: 'Get the ball; get it into space; get to it first.' In other words, if a team has the ball, they can attack, and if they attack, they can score. Greenwood's way of thinking produced the modern concept of 'total rugby', in which all 15 players are involved in the game at all times, ready to attack or defend in any situation.

Determination is written on the face of Argentina's Omar Hasan as he charges at his Australian opponents during a match in 2003.

Fair play

Playing the game hard does not mean playing dirty. Players should respect their opponents and stay within the spirit and rules of rugby, even though they are trying to beat them. And whether they win or lose, they should forget any hostility when the final whistle blows and treat the other side sportingly.

Sporting behaviour should also include attitudes towards the match officials. Referees and linesmen are bound to make mistakes occasionally, but their decisions must always be respected without question. Over a period of time, bad luck and good luck will even themselves out.

The haka

Before every international game, the New Zealand All Blacks team performs a 'haka'. This dance was used long ago by the Maori (native New Zealanders) before they went into battle. Nowadays, the haka is intended to frighten the opposition. The players stand in their half of the field, facing the other team. The ceremony includes chanting Maori words, slapping hands and chest, stamping their feet and sticking out their tongues – in time with each other. The haka ends with the whole team leaping into the air.

Leading a side

The captain of a rugby union team is its central figure. He or she may not decide the strategy, but they set the standard for the rest of the team to follow. The captain is often the best player in the side, and should show everyone what is best for the team. He or she must lead from the front, and communicate **tactics** and playing decisions. Good leaders come in all shapes and sizes, and from all positions. Among the greatest have been a **hooker** (New Zealander Sean Fitzpatrick), a second row **forward** (England's Martin Johnson) and a full-back (Scotland's Gavin Hastings).

A captain's duties

The captain is in charge of the team on the field. It is his or her responsibility to make sure that their teammates play in a disciplined and sporting manner. They make decisions about individual pieces of play (which end to play from, whether or not to take a penalty kick at goal). They are usually aided by two other important players, the leader of the forwards and the **scrum** half.

Captains also lead the players when they are off the field. They represent not only their team, but also the club or country, and will be judged by the way they behave. A captain must be prepared to speak in public at dinners and presentations, and also give interviews to the press. This is an especially important job if a team is on tour abroad.

*Led by captain George Gregan, the Australian team walks out into the field before the start of a **Test** match against South Africa.*

Selecting the team

The coach has the biggest say in choosing players for the team, but the captain's views are also very important. They should first of all decide what kind of team they want (attacking or defensive, for example), then examine each position on the field. What is needed? Are there suitable players to fill them? Every team and every match are different, so selection is a serious process.

Of course, the coach has to select the captain in the first place. Coaches may test out possible leaders by giving them responsible roles during training and seeing how they perform. They are looking for someone who is happy to represent them on the field, and will make sure that their game plans are carried out.

John Eales

Australian skipper John Eales was known to his teammates as 'Nobody' – from the common saying 'Nobody's perfect'. His quest for perfection made him one of the best and most successful rugby union captains there has ever been. Eales led Australia in 52 Tests between 1996 and 2001, winning a record 39 of them, plus every major trophy available (including the 1999 World Cup). An outstanding **lineout** jumper and kicker, he inspired his team to several great comebacks when they were in danger of defeat.

Club rugby

Club rugby union is the foundation of the game. Every single international player will have started their career at a local club – perhaps at Mini Rugby, or as a junior – and made their way up to the first team. There they will have learned what it is like to play the grown-up game, and about the dedication which is needed throughout the season. The club game is also the natural midway point between schools or Junior Rugby, and reaching the top of the profession at **Test** level.

The way up

The first step is to get noticed. Promising school or college players will certainly be approached by clubs with offers to join their squads. Others will make their way up through the club system, playing first for the age-group teams, then for the reserves and finally for the first team. There they will have to prove that they are dedicated to the life of a professional player, training hard and keeping fit.

Until the professional era, club sides would be largely made up of local players, who lived and had jobs nearby. Today, the major clubs buy in many of their stars from outside the area – and sometimes even from the other side of the world. The growth of the transfer market has often meant that the richest clubs are able to buy the best players. This makes it more difficult for other sides to compete with the same success.

Play gets under way between English club sides Bath and Saracens, amid the elegant surroundings of Bath's home ground.

Va'aiga Tuigamala

Blockbusting centre Va'aiga (Inga) Tuigamala caused a sensation in 1998 when he became rugby union's first million pound player when he was bought by Newcastle in England. He had come a long way. Born in Manu Samoa, an island group in the Pacific, he had moved to New Zealand as a child.

His talent won him an All Black debut in 1991, but he went back to represent his native land in 1996. From there he was signed up by English rugby league side Wigan, scoring 25 **tries** in his first season. Then he made his record-breaking transfer to the Newcastle rugby union side, immediately helping the team to championship success by winning the premiership.

Where does the money come from?

Modern clubs need a large and steady supply of cash – to pay the players and coaching staff, and to rent and maintain their grounds and equipment. This money comes mostly from three sources. The first is the public. Spectators pay to watch games, to become club members, and to buy merchandise such as team shirts and programmes.

The second source is the chairmen or owners. Many clubs are owned or run by people who have had a successful career outside the sport, and want to spend their money supporting their favourite club. For instance Nigel Wray, the benefactor of English club Saracens, has probably spent more than £12 million of his own money.

The third source is sponsorship. A huge number of clubs receive payments from commercial companies for advertising their names on team clothes, posters and programmes – even the pitch itself. Look at any club player, junior or international, and you will see a company name and logo on their shirt.

The national team

The ambition of every rugby player is to represent their country. International matches are the ultimate contests, both for teams and for spectators. Of the thousands of people who play for club teams, only a few will ever pull on their country's jersey. For instance, France have been playing internationals for well over 100 years, and in that time only about 800 Frenchmen have appeared in the first team.

The military band is scarcely out of the way before the Welsh team runs onto the field at the Millennium Stadium in Cardiff in 1999, led by their captain Rob Howley (with ball).

First match nerves

Internationals demand a lot more of players than even the toughest club game. For a start there is the emotional pressure. The **Test** squad of possible players usually meets weeks before the game, to sharpen their skills, discuss **tactics** and get to know each other. This can be a hard time for new players, who will be mixing with far more experienced teammates who already have established reputations.

Those who are selected for the final fifteen have more nervous moments to get over. Tension is built up by media coverage in the press, TV and radio.

Going to the ground and waiting in the dressing room is followed by the biggest moment – running onto the pitch. The size and thunderous noise of the crowd (which might be well over 70,000 strong) can be a huge shock to inexperienced players.

Mental and physical toughness

For many players, the game itself passes in a blur. As one-time Scotland captain David Sole remembered, 'One moment you're in the dressing room getting ready to come out and then,

The Lions

For players from England, Wales, Ireland or Scotland, the very greatest honour is to be picked for the Lions. This combined squad, made up of the very best from those four countries, makes regular tours of New Zealand, Australia and South Africa. The Lions play matches against major local sides, as well as a 3- or 4-Test series against the host nation. They have had a particularly difficult time in New Zealand, where they have won only 6 matches and lost 24 since the first tour in 1904!

hey presto, it's all over and you're back in the dressing room again.' A successful debut may lead to more appearances, but this does not mean that the nerves will disappear. Several veteran players are always physically sick on the morning before an international match.

Toughness is shown in other ways. There is the physical strength which can stand up to the battering of a dozen Test matches a year, as well as 30 or more club games. And there is the mental strength, to cope with the pressure of responsibility and publicity.

Joe Rokocoko

Joe Rokocoko had the difficult task of replacing Jonah Lomu in the New Zealand team in 2003. Yet the 20-year-old wing quickly showed that he was just as great a player. His lightning pace and long strides brought him eleven tries in his first seven Tests. Like Lomu, he is a Pacific islander, being born in Fiji and moving to New Zealand at the age of five.

The World Cup

Which is the best side in the world? This question is settled by the Rugby World Cup competition, which takes place in a different host country every four years, and draws an enormous audience worldwide, at the grounds and on television. For many coaches and players, this is the target they are aiming at, and they spend the period in between preparing a team to win the Cup.

World Cup history

The first World Cup was held in Australia and New Zealand in 1987. Sixteen countries took part, including Japan, Zimbabwe, Tonga and the USA. New Zealand won the cup very easily, having scored nearly 300 points during the competition. The second contest, in the UK, Ireland and France four years later, was much closer. This time Australia won a tense final against England.

A delighted England skipper Martin Johnson holds up the World Cup after his team had won the final match against Australia in Sydney in 2003.

South Africa were hosts in 1995, celebrating their return to world rugby union after being excluded during the repressive **apartheid** era of the 1970s and 1980s. Their victory in the final over New Zealand was hugely popular. The competition returned to the UK, Ireland and France in 1999, with 20 teams taking part. Australia won the cup for the second time. Australia hosted the 2003 World Cup. A late drop goal by England's Jonny Wilkinson secured a 20-17 extra-time win in the final against the Wallabies.

England scrum half Matt Dawson throws out a pass during the 2003 World Cup semi-final against France.

Getting to the final

Before the actual World Cup Finals come the qualifying rounds, in which the non-**Test** playing countries compete against each other. This early stage involves over 60 teams from Europe, Oceania, the Americas, Africa and Asia. Only twelve of these can qualify for the final stages, where they join the eight top-ranked sides.

For the tournament itself, the teams are divided into five 'pools', and the four teams in each play each other once. The five teams that come out top of the pools go on to the quarter finals. The teams that come second or third then play each other to decide who will be the other three quarter-finalists. Eventually, after quarter-finals and semi-finals, the two best sides meet in the final.

South Africa's President Nelson Mandela presents the World Cup to Francois Pienaar, captain of the winning South African team in Johannesburg in 1995.

Being a champion

Getting to be a top rugby union player is not easy. It involves long hours of dedicated skills and fitness training, which drives even the best athletes to their limits. They may become celebrities, with their own TV slots and newspaper columns, and may be recognized in the street and pestered in bars. In rugby-mad countries such as New Zealand and Australia they may even have their own websites and fan clubs.

Signing autographs is one of the chores of the famous rugby player. Here South African Victor Matfield signs a cap for a young fan during the 2003 World Cup in Perth, Australia.

Staying at the top

Staying on top is even harder. Fame builds up the pressure on players to go on performing at exceptionally high standards. An international career can stretch over ten years, and include 100 **Test** matches. That is over 130 hours of high-intensity, bone-shaking rugby, and only a very good and exceptionally strong player can last such a long time.

The biggest challenge is keeping up fitness and form. Constant impacts from tackling, and the twisting and turning of running and mauling, may cause lasting damage to joints and limbs. The punishing training routine becomes more difficult year after year. Irish hooker Keith Wood suffered twelve months of neck and shoulder problems before coming back to play in the 2003 World Cup. A player will also have periods out of form, when skills and enthusiasm fall below the usual high standard. These problems can be cured by individual coaching sessions, or by consulting a psychologist who will improve focus and motivation.

End of a career

A champion rugby player's life at the top can be very short. Very few go on playing internationals after their early thirties, and most retire from top-class club rugby at about the same time. Retirement can often be a shock for people who have been used to fame, excitement and regular physical exertion. Some retired players become administrators, helping to run clubs and other rugby organizations. Some (like Scotland's Ian McGeechan) become coaches, handing on their experience and knowledge to younger people. A few work as commentators on radio and television, or specialist journalists for newspapers.

The final curtain. The great Australian wing David Campese leaves the field after his last match, playing against the Barbarians at Twickenham in 1996.

Brian O'Driscoll

Few rugby players have soared to superstardom as quickly as Ireland's Brian O'Driscoll. He began the game at the age of twelve at his Dublin school, and by seventeen was playing for the Irish Schools team. He featured in the Ireland Under-19 side which won a world title, and made his international debut at twenty. Since then he has scored a record 18 **tries** for his country in 41 Tests, including two hat-tricks

(sets of three tries in one match), and been appointed captain. O'Driscoll's try for the British Lions against Australia in 2001 is reckoned to be one of the best ever seen. But he is still ambitious, insisting 'I want to go out and win things with Ireland. I don't want to be part of a nearly team.'

International rugby records

Records are an important part of rugby, but they do not play such a central role as they do in, for example, cricket or athletics. The figures here show who has scored most points or played in most games or excelled in other parts of the sport. Most of them have been set since about 1980. This is because there are many more international matches each year for players to take part in, so they have a greater chance of breaking records than those of previous periods.

World Cup Records		
Record	**Amount**	**Record Holder/s**
Most successful country		Australia (winners 1991, 1999, finalists 2003)
Most points in a match	145	by New Zealand v Japan 1995
Most points in World Cup final stages	227	by Gavin Hastings (Scotland) 1987–95
Most tries in World Cup final stages	15	by Jonah Lomu (New Zealand) 1995–99
Most points in one competition	126	by Grant Fox (New Zealand) 1987
Most tries in one competition	8	by Jonah Lomu (New Zealand) 1999
Most tries in a match	6	by M.C.G. Ellis, New Zealand v Japan 1995
Most penalty goals in a match	8	by Matt Burke, Australia v South Africa 1999
Most drop goals in a match	5	by Jannie de Beer, South Africa v England 1999

Men's Team Records		
Record	**Amount**	**Team/Match/Year**
Most consecutive victories	17	New Zealand 1965–69
		South Africa 1997–98
		England 2002–03
Most points in a match	155	Japan v Taipei, 2002
Most tries in a match	24	Argentina v Paraguay, 2002
Most penalty goals in a match	9	Japan v Tonga, 1999

Male Player Records		
Record	Amount	Player/Country/Match/Year
Most points in a match	60	T. Kurihara, Japan v Taipei 2002
Most points in a Test career	1070	Neil Jenkins (Wales) 1991–2002
Most tries in a match	8	G.M. Jorge, Argentina v Brazil 1993
		D. Ohata, Japan v Taipei 2002
Most tries in a Test career	64	David Campese (Australia) 1982–96
Most conversions in a match	20	S.D. Culhane, New Zealand v Japan 1995
Most conversions in a Test career	154	Andrew Mehrtens* (New Zealand) 1995–2003
Most penalty goals in a match	9	K. Hirose, Japan v Tonga 1999
		Andrew Mehrtens, New Zealand v Australia 1999
		New Zealand v France 2000
		Neil Jenkins, Wales v France 1999
Most penalty goals in a Test career	244	Neil Jenkins (Wales) 1991–2002
Most drop goals in a match	5	Jannie de Beer, South Africa v England 1999
Most drop goals in a Test career	28	Hugo Porta (Argentina) 1971–90
Most capped players	111	Philippe Sella (France) 1982–95
	114	Jason Leonard (England) 1990–2003
Most consecutive Tests	63	Sean Fitzpatrick (New Zealand) 1986–95
Most Tests as captain	59	Will Carling (England) 1988–96
		*still playing

Women's rugby facts

The first women's international was between Great Britain and France in 1986.

England's first-ever match was against Wales in 1987, with the English winning 22–4.

The first women's World Cup was held in Cardiff in 1991. The USA beat England 19–6 in the final.

England got revenge over the USA in the 1994 final in Edinburgh, winning 38–23. New Zealand won the third tournament, also beating the USA in the final.

There is now also a women's Six Nations, involving England, Scotland, Wales, Ireland, France and Spain.

Statistics in this book were correct on 1 May 2004

Glossary

apartheid
the policy of racial separation of black, Asian and white peoples, made law in South Africa from the late 1940s to the early 1990s

backs
the players who stand behind the scrum

binding
holding onto another player with the arm to form a scrum

forwards
the players who form the scrum

front row
the first row of the scrum, consisting of a hooker and two props

half volley
a kick made just as the ball touches the ground

hand off
the ball-carrier using the arm or hand to push away an opponent

hooker
player at the centre of the front row of the scrum who 'hooks' or guides the ball back with his feet

lineout
the throw-in of the ball from touch to lines of forwards

peeling
catching the ball and carrying it round the tail of the line in a lineout in close formation

props
players in the front row of the scrum who 'prop' or support the hooker

punt
a kick of the ball made straight from the hand to the boot

scissors
a pass to a player who is running at a different angle

scrum
a) a collective name for the forwards
b) a pushing contest between two sets of eight opposing forwards, bound to each other

set-piece
a set way of restarting a game, such as a kick-off or lineout

tactics
a team's plan for beating the opposition

technique
a skill or a systematic way of doing something

Test
game between two international teams

touch
the lines marking the edge, at the sides of the pitch: if a ball or player touches the line, they are 'in touch'

try
the grounding of the ball by a player in the opponents' in-goal area

up-and-under
a high kick up field for one's own players to chase and get 'under'

Resources

Further reading

International Rugby Yearbook, Mick Cleary and John Griffith (Collins Willow, 2003)
An annual guide to the events, personalities and records of the previous year.

Rugby: A Player's Guide to the Laws, Derek Robinson (Harper Collins, 2002)
The laws of the game, clearly explained.

Rugby Skills, Tactics and Rules: The New Zealand Way, Tony Williams and Gordon Hunter (Gill & Macmillan, 2000)
A lavishly illustrated guide to rugby basics in the All Black style.

Useful websites and adresses

England Rugby Football Union
Rugby House
Rugby Road
Twickenham TW1 1DS
ENGLAND
www.rfu.com

Irish Rugby Football Union
62 Lansdowne Road
Ballsbridge
Dublin 4
EIRE
www.irishrugby.ie

Scottish Rugby Football Union
Murrayfield
Edinburgh EH12 5PJ
SCOTLAND
www.scottishrugby.org

Welsh Rugby Union
Custom House Street
Cardiff CF10 1RF
WALES
www.wru.co.uk

Australian Rugby Union
181 Miller Street
North Sydney NSW 2060
AUSTRALIA
www.rugby.com.au

New Zealand Rugby Football Union
1 Hinemoa Street
Centrepoint
PO Box 2172
Wellington
NEW ZEALAND
www.nzrugby.com

South African Rugby Football Union
Boundary Road
PO Box 99
Newlands
Cape Town 7725
SOUTH AFRICA
www.sarugby.net

International Rugby Board
Huguenot House
35–38 St Stephen's Green
Dublin 2
EIRE
www.irb.com

Disclaimer

All the Internet addresses (URLs) given in this book were valid at the time of going to press. However, due to the dynamic nature of the Internet, some addresses may have changed, or sites may have changed or ceased to exist since publication. While the author and Publishers regret any inconvenience this may cause readers, no responsibility for any such changes can be accepted by either the author or the Publishers.

Index

Titles in the *Making of a Champion* series include:

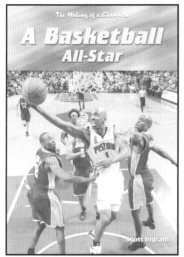

Hardback   0 431 18938 2

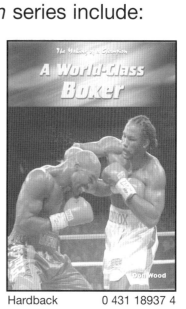

Hardback   0 431 18937 4

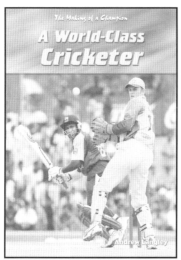

Hardback   0 431 18940 4

Hardback   0 431 18936 6

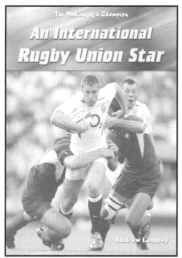

Hardback   0 431 18939 0

Hardback   0 431 18935 8

Find out about the other titles in this series on our website www.heinemann.co.uk/library